Come to the Carnival

Festival Poems

Chosen by John Foster

OXFORD
UNIVERSITY PRESS

OXFORD
UNIVERSITY PRESS

Great Clarendon Street, Oxford OX2 6DP

Oxford University Press is a department of the University of Oxford.
It furthers the University's objective of excellence in research, scholarship,
and education by publishing worldwide in

Oxford New York

Athens Auckland Bangkok Bogotá Buenos Aires
Cape Town Chennai Dar es Salaam Delhi Florence Hong Kong Istanbul
Karachi Kolkata Kuala Lumpur Madrid Melbourne Mexico City Mumbai
Nairobi Paris São Paulo Shanghai Singapore Taipei Tokyo Toronto
Warsaw

with associated companies in Berlin Ibadan

Oxford is a registered trade mark of Oxford University Press
in the UK and in certain other countries

British Library Cataloguing in Publication Data available

ISBN 0 19 2762869
10 9 8 7 6 5 4 3 2 1

Printed in China

We are grateful to the authors for permission to reprint the following poems.

First published in John Foster (ed.): *Steelband Jump Up* (OUP, 2000):
Faustin Charles: 'Steelband Jump Up', © Faustin Charles 2000; **Nigel Gray:**
'Sharing' adapted from a traditional Sudanese poem, © Nigel Gray 2000.

First published in John Foster (ed.): *Come to the Carnival* (OUP, 2000):

Debjani Chatterjee: 'Diwali', © Debjani Chatterjee 2000; **Jean Kenward:**
'May Day', © Jean Kenward 2000; **John Kitching:** 'Birthday', © John
Kitching 2000; **Tony Langham:** 'Eid Song', © Tony Langham 2000; **Erica
Stewart:** 'Come to the Carnival', © Erica Stewart 2000.

We are also grateful for permission to reprint the following poems:

John Agard: 'I Like to Squeeze' from *Get Back, Pimple!* (Viking Kestrel, 1996),
reprinted by permission of Caroline Sheldon Literary Agency on behalf of
the author; **Giles Andreae:** 'Chimpanzee' from *Rumble in the Jungle* by
permission of the publisher, Orchard Books, a division of The Watts
Publishing Group Limited; **Moira Andrew:** 'November Riddle' first published
in *Curriculum Bank Poetry KS2* by Moira Andrew (Scholastic Publications,
1999), © Moira Andrew 1999, reprinted by permission of the author; **Faustin
Charles:** 'Through the Jungle the Elephant Goes' from *The Kiskadee Queen*
(Blackie), reprinted by permission of the author; **Leonard Clark:** 'Harvest
Home', reprinted by permission of the Literary Executor of Leonard Clark;
Eleanor Farjeon: 'Advice to a Child' from *The Children's Bells* (OUP, 1957),
reprinted by permission of David Higham Associates; **Max Fatchen:** 'And
Behind Your Ears, Too' from *Peculiar Rhymes and Lunatic Lines* (Orchard,
1995), reprinted by permission of John Johnson (Authors' Agent) Ltd; **John
Foster:** 'Chinese New Year Dragon' from *Bouncing Ben and Other Rhymes*,
(OUP, 1998), © John Foster 1998, reprinted by permission of the author;
Grace Nichols: 'The Sun' from *Come On Into My Tropical Garden* (A & C
Black, 1988), © Grace Nichols 1988, reprinted by permission of Curtis Brown
Ltd, London, on behalf of the author; **James Reeves:** 'Fireworks', © James
Reeves from *Complete Poems for Children* (Heinemann), reprinted by
permission of the James Reeves Estate, c/o Laura Cecil Literary Agency.

Despite efforts to obtain permission from all copyright holders before
publication, this has not been possible in a few cases. If notified the
publisher will be pleased to rectify any errors or omissions at the earliest
opportunity.

The illustrations are by:
Basia Bogdanowicz pp. 6–7; Tim Clarey pp. 14–15; Steve Cox pp. 10–11;
Rebecca Gryspeerdt p. 25; Charlotte Hard p. 17;
Jan McCafferty pp. 8–9; Alan Marks p. 28; Mrinal Mitra p. 29; Kaoru Miyake
p. 16; Yvonne Muller pp. 18–19;
Lindy Norton pp. 22–23; Petra Rohr-Rouendaal pp. 20–21, 32; Evie
Safarewicz pp. 4–5; Emma Shaw-Smith pp. 30–31;
Thomas Taylor pp. 26–27; Kay Widdowson pp. 12–13, 24

List of contents:

Come to the Carnival

Come to the Carnival.
Hear the steelbands play.
Come to the Carnival.
It's Carnival Day today.

Dress up like a peacock.
Dress up like a king.
Dress up like a monkey.
Clap your hands and sing.

Dance like a princess.
Tumble like a clown.
Stamp your feet to the beat,
Swaying up and down.

Come to the Carnival.
Hear the steelbands play.
Come to the Carnival.
It's Carnival Day today.

Erica Stewart

Lizzie

Lizzie, Lizzie, spinning top,
Ever dancing, never stop.
Dancing in the morning dew,
Barefoot tap, one two, one two.

Lizzie, Lizzie, spinning top,
Ever dancing, never stop.
Dancing in the sun's warm rays,
Shining brightly at midday.

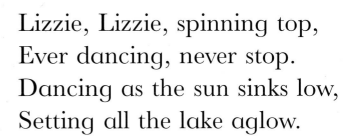

Lizzie, Lizzie, spinning top,
Ever dancing, never stop.
Dancing as the sun sinks low,
Setting all the lake aglow.

Now she's lying in her bed.
Rosy pillow 'neath her head.
Round the fence a dream comes creeping.
Softly now...for Lizzie's sleeping.

Traditional Polish

Pancakes

Mummy made pancakes on Tuesday
She tossed them in the air
One fell on the floor
Two fell on the chair
One fell on the cooker
One fell on the grate
But lucky me I got three
Because they fell on my plate.

Glenn O'Neill (8 years)

May Day

Twirl your ribbons
    as you go
in and out
    the Maypole...
Let the colours
    twist and flow
in and out
    the Maypole!

Skip and follow,
    turn about,
round and round
    the Maypole!
Outside in
    and inside out –
round and round
    the Maypole!

Jean Kenward

9

The Kangaroo

Old Jumpety-Bumpety-Hop-and-Go-One
Was lying asleep on his side in the sun.
This old kangaroo, he was whisking the flies
(With his long glossy tail) from his ears and his eyes.
Jumpety-Bumpety-Hop-and-Go-One
Was lying asleep on his side in the sun.
Jumpety-Bumpety-Hop!

Traditional Australian

Ole Grandpa Jake

Ole Grandpa Jake,
Changed into a snake,
He bit he own tail,
An' started to wail.

Traditional West Indian

Chinese New Year Dragon

There's a brightly coloured dragon,
swaying down the street,
stomping and stamping
and kicking up its feet.

There's a multi-coloured dragon,
– green and gold and red –
twisting and twirling
and shaking its head.

There's a silky-scaled dragon,
parading through the town,
swishing and swooshing
and rippling up and down.

There's a swirling, whirling dragon,
weaving to and fro,
prancing and dancing
and putting on a show.

There's cheering and clapping,
as the dragon draws near –
a sign of good luck
and a happy new year!

John Foster

Sampan

Waves lap lap
Fish fins clap clap
Brown sails flap flap
Chop-sticks tap tap
Up and down the long green river
Ohe Ohe lanterns quiver
Willow branches brush the river
Ohe Ohe lanterns quiver
Waves lap lap
Fish fins clap clap
Brown sails flap flap
Chop-sticks tap tap

Tao Lang Pee

The Sun

The sun is a glowing spider
that crawls out
from under the earth
to make her way across the sky
warming and weaving
with her bright old fingers
of light.

Grace Nichols

Rain Song

The small rain,
The long rain,
The lasting rain,
Rain! Rain!
Oh, Rain God
Water our Earth.

Traditional Polynesian

Birthday

Birthday, birthday!
First day on earth day.
Full of joy and mirth day.
Wonderment and worth day.
Very happy birthday.
Glad to be on earth day.

John Kitching

The Wish

Each birthday wish
I've ever made
Really does come true.
Each year I wish
I'll grow some more
And every year
   I
      DO!

Ann Friday

Steelband Jump Up

I put my ear to the ground,
And I hear the steelband sound:
Ping pong! Ping pong!
Music deep, rhythm sweet,
I'm dancing tracking the beat;
Like a sea-shell's ringing song,
Ping pong! Ping pong!
Moving along, moving along.
High and low, up and down,
Ping pong! Ping pong!
Pan beating singing, round and round,
Ping pong! Ping pong!

Faustin Charles

Sharing

My mother gave me water,
I gave the water to the earth.
The earth gave me grass,
I gave the grass to the cow.
The cow gave me milk,
I gave the milk to the baker.
The baker gave me fire,
I gave the fire to the blacksmith.
The blacksmith gave me scissors,
I gave the scissors to the tailor.
The tailor gave me a coat,
I gave the coat to the farmer.
The farmer gave me dates,
I shared the dates with my mother.
My mother gave me water,
and said, "Bless you, my daughter."

Traditional Sudanese adapted by Nigel Gray

20

November Riddle

We scribble on the dark
with felt-tip pens,
weave patterns in the air
and roar like dragons.

We bloom and fade and fall,
our short lives
scattered over the earth
in a silver fall of sparks.

Moira Andrew

Fireworks

They rise like sudden fiery flowers
    That burst upon the night,
Then fall to earth in burning showers
    Of crimson, blue and white.

Like buds too wonderful to name,
    Each miracle unfolds,
And catherine-wheels begin to flame
    Like whirling marigolds.

Rockets and Roman candles make
    An orchard of the sky,
Whence magic trees their petals shake
    Upon each gazing eye.

James Reeves

Harvest Home

Wheat is all cut.
Oats safe in bags,
Barley just ripe,
Tractor zig-zags
Bumping downhill
Trailer with beans
And at the wheel
Girl in blue jeans,
In orchard below,
Baskets of plums
Wait under trees
Till fruit lorry comes.
Harvest is in.
And home go the growers,
The pickers, the mowers;
Let dancing begin
At the end of day
Now harvest is in.

Leonard Clark

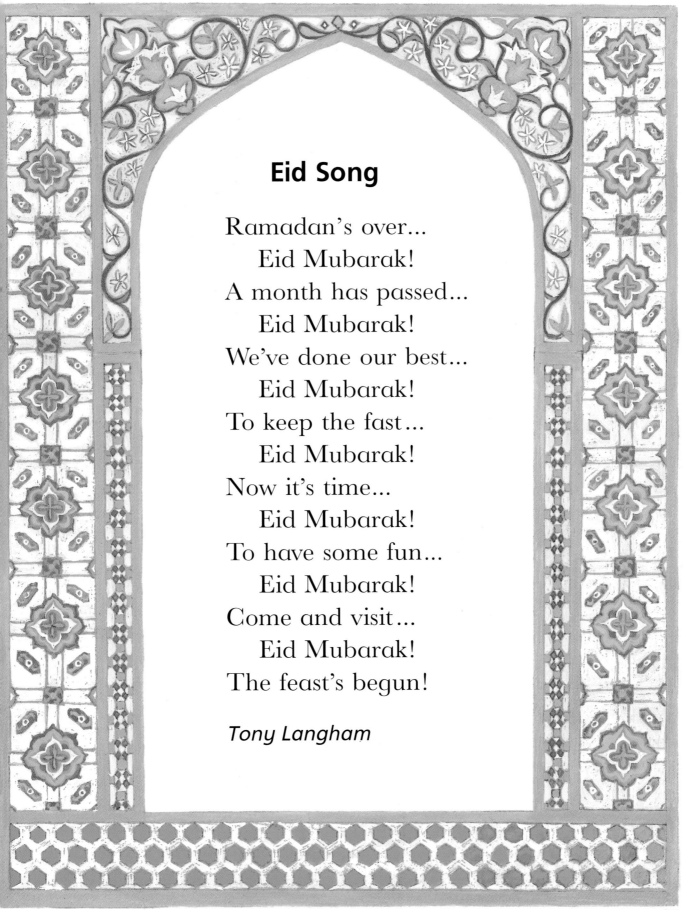

Eid Song

Ramadan's over...
    Eid Mubarak!
A month has passed...
    Eid Mubarak!
We've done our best...
    Eid Mubarak!
To keep the fast...
    Eid Mubarak!
Now it's time...
    Eid Mubarak!
To have some fun...
    Eid Mubarak!
Come and visit...
    Eid Mubarak!
The feast's begun!

Tony Langham

Through the Jungle the Elephant Goes

Through the jungle the elephant goes,
Swaying his trunk to and fro,
Munching, crunching, tearing trees,
Stamping seeds, eating leaves.
His eyes are small, his feet are fat.
Hey, elephant, don't behave like that.

Traditional Indian

Chimpanzee

It's great to be a chimpanzee
Swinging through the trees
And if we can't find nuts to eat
We munch each other's fleas!

Giles Andreae

And Behind Your Ears, Too

A mother hippopotamus,
Her voice both calm and steady,
Said, "Do come here,
It's bath-time dear.
I've got your river ready."

Max Fatchen

The Whisper-Whisper Man

The Whisper-Whisper Man
Makes all the wind in the world.
He has a gown as brown as brown;
His hair is long and curled.

In the stormy winter time
He taps at your window-pane.
And all the night, until it's light,
He whispers through the rain.

If you peeped through a Fairy Ring
You'd see him, little and brown;
You'd hear the beat of his clackety feet
Scampering through the town.

Traditional Irish

Diwali

Diwali lamps are twinkling, twinkling
In the sky and in our homes and hearts.
We welcome all with cheery greetings
And sweets and patterned *rangoli* art.
Lakshmi flies upon her owl tonight;
Incense curls, our future's sparkling bright.

Debjani Chatterjee

Advice to a Child

Set your fir-tree
In a pot;
Needles green
Is all it's got.
Shut the door
And go away,
And so to sleep
Till Christmas Day.
In the morning
Seek your tree,
And you shall see
What you shall see.

Hang your stocking
By the fire,
Empty of
Your heart's desire.
Up the chimney
Say your say,
And so to sleep
Till Christmas Day.
In the morning
Draw the blind,
And you shall find
What you shall find.

Eleanor Farjeon

I'd Like to Squeeze

I'd like to squeeze this round world
into a new shape

I'd like to squeeze this round world
like a tube of toothpaste

I'd like to squeeze this round world
fair and square

I'd like to squeeze it and squeeze it
till everybody had an equal share

John Agard